CPH TEACHING RESOURCE

GRADES
4-6

# Super Songs for Christ's Kids

## 20 songs plus creative music activities

**CPH**
Concordia Publishing House

Editor: Tom Nummela

Your comments and suggestions concerning this material are appreciated. Please write the Sunday School Editor, Concordia Publishing House, 3558 S. Jefferson Avenue, St. Louis, MO 63118-3968.

This publication is also available in Braille and in large type for the visually impaired. Call 1-800-433-3954 or write to Library for the Blind, 1333 S. Kirkwood Rd., St. Louis, MO 63122-7295.

1    2    3    4    5    6    7    8    9    10              08    07    06    05    04    03    02    01    00    99

# Contents

# Songs in Alphabetical Order

(First page number indicates the song with accompaniment; the second number indicates the song lyrics.)

# Introduction

Psalm 150 closes the church's first songbook with these words, *"Let everything that has breath praise the LORD"* (v. 6). This admonition to praise God is all-inclusive. Certainly, all God's people, young and old, are encouraged to voice their thanks and adoration to our Lord and Savior for all His wonderful blessings. *Super Songs for Christ's Kids* is a unique resource for such thanksgiving and praise. This book will provide fourth through sixth graders with excellent songs and exciting activities with which they can praise the Lord.

Sunday school teachers, day school teachers, song leaders, and others who work with children's music in churches and Christian schools will find this book especially useful for several reasons:

- It brings together in one volume songs from several sources. Some are brand-new songs, others are popular songs recently published by CPH for VBS, and several are popular songs published by others. Each was chosen for its appeal to children in grades four through six and those who often lead them in singing.
- For each song, several activities are provided that will help music leaders and teachers teach and lead the songs in ways that will get the children involved and enthused. These activities range from ideas for singing in parts to discussions to help children reflect on and better understand the lyrics.
- Song texts have been included on easy-to-reproduce pages in the back of the book. The purchaser of this book has permission to copy the lyrics for group singing.
- All 20 songs are available on compact disk or audiocassette in *two* versions—one that includes sung lyrics and one that includes only the accompaniment. Use the vocal recording to introduce the songs and support your singers as they learn them. Use the accompaniment recording when the song is familiar to your group. (On the CD, the vocal versions are on Disc 1; the accompaniment versions are are on Disc 2. On the audiocassette, the vocal and accompaniment versions are on opposite sides of the cassette.)

As you introduce these songs to your students, here are some suggestions for success:

1. Learn the song well. Listen to the recording several times. Sing along. Memorize the song if you can (with most of these songs that will not be hard). If you are able, also learn the keyboard accompaniment, or at least the melody, so you can help the children learn the song easily.

2.  Review the suggested activities and choose those that best fit your group. Some will require pulling together special resources—plan ahead. Remember that the activities that are suggested for one song may very well work with others. It may help to review the entire book.

3.  With some songs, it is easiest to learn the melody and text separately. First speak the text together and review any difficult pronunciations. Then speak it together in rhythm, without worrying about the melody. Then learn the melody—first listening to it played on the keyboard, then singing it softly along with the music using a neutral syllable such as "doo," then singing the text softly as the music or recording is played. Once the song as been learned, experiment with options such as antiphonal singing or additional parts.

4.  Encourage memorization. The best singing occurs when the singers are confident and know the song well. Hand motions and posters with pictures or key words can be useful in the process of memorizing.

Psalm 96 says it well:

*Sing to the LORD a new song;*
*     sing to the LORD, all the earth.*
*Sing to the LORD, praise His name;*
*     proclaim His salvation day after day.*
Psalm 96:1–2
Enjoy these "new songs" of praise.

# 1. Celebrate Jesus!

Based on Psalm 33

L. H.

Lisa Hahn

*Chorus*

Let's cel - e-brate (come on and cel - e-brate), Let's cel - e-brate (come on and cel-e-brate),

**1, 2, 3**     **4**

Let's cel - e-brate (Shout for joy and)— Cel-e-brate Je-sus!

*Verse*

1. Sing to Him, you joy - ful ones; Make mu - sic, play, and shout. He's
2. By His Word the earth was formed; He made the sea and sky. He
3. His love for us does - n't end. His words are right and true. A
4. So we wait in hope for Him; Our help and shield He'll be. In

made you righ - teous in His sight, So let your praise come out!
sent His Son to pay for sin So we can live on high.
love that will not fail or fade— A love for me and you!
Him our hearts re - joice and sing 'Cause Christ has set us free!

> *Sing joyfully to the LORD, you righteous;*
> *it is fitting for the upright to praise Him …*
> *We wait in hope for the LORD;*
> *He is our help and our shield.*
> *In Him our hearts rejoice,*
> *for we trust in His holy name.*
> Psalm 33:1, 20–22

# Let's Celebrate!

## Activities for Involving Children
**("Celebrate Jesus!" is found on page 7.)**

Invite the children to participate in a "popcorn" prayer. Begin by saying, "Thanks, Lord, for all Your gifts." Then let the children "pop" in with the things they are thankful for and happy about today. Conclude by saying, "Thanks for giving us faith in Your Son. Help us celebrate Your love always. Amen."

As you teach and sing this song, have part of the group learn the antiphonal phrases of the refrain (in parentheses) and sing them **boldly**.

Distribute blank paper and your choice of art supplies. Encourage the students to study Psalm 148 (you may make copies of the text printed below) and illustrate any portion of the psalm by showing how various parts of God's creation praise Him.

Have the children locate Psalm 33 in their Bibles. Challenge them to discover the verses of the psalm upon which the stanzas of the song are based.

## Psalm 148

¹Praise the LORD.
    Praise the LORD from the heavens,
    praise Him in the heights above.
²Praise Him, all His angels,
    praise Him, all His heavenly hosts.
³Praise Him, sun and moon,
    praise Him, all you shining stars.
⁴Praise Him, you highest heavens
    and you waters above the skies.
⁵Let them praise the name of the LORD,
    for He commanded and they were
    created.
⁶He set them in place for ever and ever;
    He gave a decree that will never
    pass away.
⁷Praise the LORD from the earth,
    you great sea creatures and all
    ocean depths,
⁸lightning and hail, snow and clouds,
    stormy winds that do His bidding,

⁹you mountains and all hills,
    fruit trees and all cedars,
¹⁰wild animals and all cattle,
    small creatures and flying birds,
¹¹kings of the earth and all nations,
    you princes and all rulers on
    earth,
¹²young men and maidens,
    old men and children.
¹³Let them praise the name of the LORD,
    for His name alone is exalted;
    His splendor is above the earth
    and the heavens.
¹⁴He has raised up for His people a
    horn,
    the praise of all His saints,
    of Israel, the people close to His
    heart.
Praise the LORD.

# 2. Don't Look Back

L. G.

Lana Gibbons

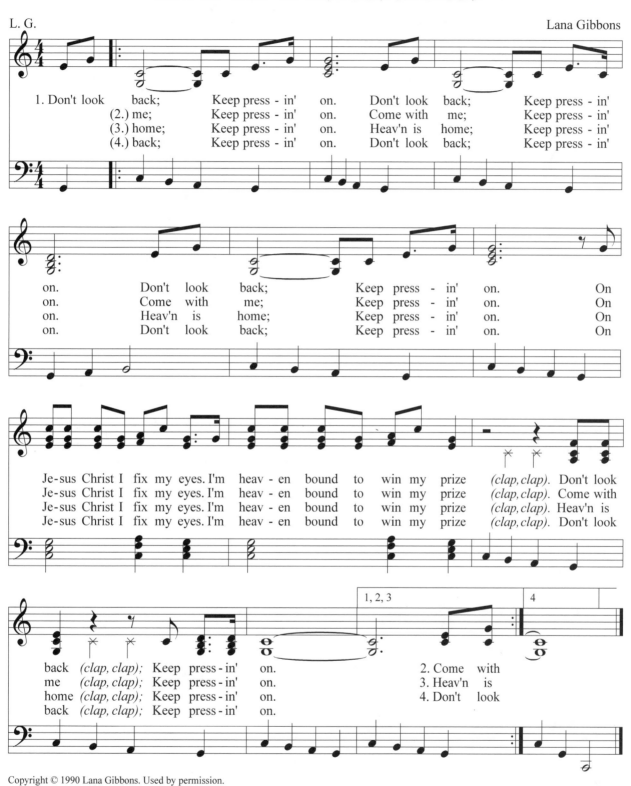

1. Don't look back; Keep press - in' on. Don't look back; Keep press - in'
(2.) me; Keep press - in' on. Come with me; Keep press - in'
(3.) home; Keep press - in' on. Heav'n is home; Keep press - in'
(4.) back; Keep press - in' on. Don't look back; Keep press - in'

on. Don't look back; Keep press - in' on. On
on. Come with me; Keep press - in' on. On
on. Heav'n is home; Keep press - in' on. On
on. Don't look back; Keep press - in' on. On

Je-sus Christ I fix my eyes. I'm heav - en bound to win my prize *(clap, clap)*. Don't look
Je-sus Christ I fix my eyes. I'm heav - en bound to win my prize *(clap, clap)*. Come with
Je-sus Christ I fix my eyes. I'm heav - en bound to win my prize *(clap, clap)*. Heav'n is
Je-sus Christ I fix my eyes. I'm heav - en bound to win my prize *(clap, clap)*. Don't look

**1, 2, 3** | **4**

back *(clap, clap)*; Keep press - in' on. 2. Come with
me *(clap, clap)*; Keep press - in' on. 3. Heav'n is
home *(clap, clap)*; Keep press - in' on. 4. Don't look
back *(clap, clap)*; Keep press - in' on.

*Forgetting what is behind and straining toward what is ahead, I press on toward the goal to win the prize for which God has called me heavenward in Christ Jesus. Philippians 3:13b–14*

### Activities for Involving Children
("Don't Look Back" is found on page 9.)

 Teach and use the claps that accentuate the last two lines of the song.

 Bring out the kazoos! Let small groups of children take turns improvising fanfares (use the notes of a C7 chord—C, E, G,B♭) and playing along on the melody.

☆ March in place. After the chil - dren have learned the words, lead them through a few drill maneuvers ("left faces" on the fourth beat of each measure or "halt, one [stop right foot], two [stop left foot]" on measures 7 or 13.

☆ Let the boys impro- vise an ostinato (a repeating pattern of notes) on the first two and last two lines ("Don't look back …"), using the notes of the bass line in the accompaniment and the words "Press-ing on, keep press-ing on, keep …" with a slightly percussive emphasis.

☆ Teach some simple actions to go with the words:

| | |
|---|---|
| Don't look back; | *Thumbs over shoulders.* |
| Keep pressin' on. | *Both hands push forward on the word <u>on</u>. (repeat as needed)* |
| | |
| On Jesus Christ | *Index finger pointing forward.* |
| I fix my eyes. | *Shade eyes with hand.* |
| I'm heaven bound | *Index finger pointing up.* |
| to win my prize. | *Hand over heart.* |
| Come with me … | *"Come here" motion with hand.* |
| Heav'n is home … | *Index finger pointing up.* |

# 3. Come and Glorify the Name

D.M.

Dana Mengel

# 3. Come and Glorify the Name—continued

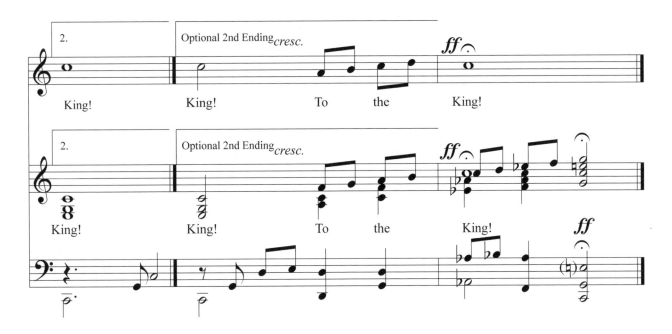

*With this in mind, we constantly pray for you, that our God may count you worthy of His calling, and that by His power He may fulfill every good purpose of yours and every act prompted by your faith. We pray this so that the name of our Lord Jesus may be glorified in you, and you in Him, according to the grace of our God and the Lord Jesus Christ.*
2 Thessalonians 1:11–12

# Come and Glorify the Name

## Activities for Involving Children

("Come and Glorify the Name" is found beginning on page 11.)

⚡ Teach a small group of singers the optional descant on the second half of the song. As an alternative, have it played on a flute or on an electronic keyboard with a flute setting.

⚡ Do a ribbon dance. Provide each child with 6 to 8 feet of wide ribbon. (The ribbon can be attached to a wooden dowel about 2 feet long for easy manipulation of the ribbons.) Let the children experiment waving the ribbons in time with the song. Try big circles, figure eights, and over the head. Then choreograph movements that all the children can do simultaneously as they sing the song.

⚡ Invite someone familiar with American Sign Language to teach the children to "speak" the words of the song in hand signs. Use the signs as a mnemonic device to remember the words. Do the hand signs together in a flowing manner as the song is sung.

# 4. Make Me Like You

L. G.

Lana Gibbons

*Gently*

*Be imitators of God, therefore, as dearly loved children, and live a life of love, just as Christ loved us and gave Himself up for us as a fragrant offering and sacrifice to God. Ephesians 5:1–2*

# Make Me Like You

✝ Invite the children to study the words of the song, picturing in their mind the specific actions of Jesus' followers that result from **WWJD—walking with Jesus daily**, by the power of the Holy Spirit. How will disciples talk? What will disciples listen to? How will disciples show they care? Whom will they forgive? Help the children to see how Jesus is at work in their lives.

✝ Direct the students to write short prayers requesting Jesus' help in specific areas of their lives. Invite volunteers to speak their prayers between stanzas as the song is sung.

✝ Remind them that this song can be a powerful reminder of Jesus' help and strength in their daily lives. When they are challenged to "live like Jesus" in difficult situations, they can sing this song, remembering its message.

# Here I Stand

## Activities for Involving Children
("Here I Stand" is found beginning on page 18.)

Invite the children to devise actions to accompany the words of the repeated section of this song. For example: "Here (point to the ground in front of you) I (point to yourself) stand (stand erect with head up and shoulders back) in worship (throw your arms straight up and slowly lower them to your sides) before God's throne," and so on.

Teach the group a cheer to be chanted before singing the song (perhaps while the music is played in the background). Here's a simple cheer:

| Here | I | stand | on the |
|------|------|------|------|
| Rock of | Jesus | Christ. | |
| Here | I | stand, | for He's |
| Given | me new | life. | |
| Grace, | faith, | Word | are the |
| Gifts He's | given | me. | |
| Here | I | stand; | His |
| Truth has | made me | free. | |

Use this song to celebrate the "birthday of the Protestant church"—Reformation Day (October 31). Point out that the repeated section reminds us of the stand taken by the reformer Martin Luther at Worms (in present-day Germany) in 1521. Luther affirmed that our salvation was God's gift to us through Jesus Christ, without any merit or work on our part—*only by grace, only through faith,* as taught *only in God's Word.* Point out these three concepts in the center section of the song.

# 5. Here I Stand

**Based on Romans 5:1–2**

L. G.

Lana Gibbons

*With great boldness!*

*Refrain:* Here I stand in wor-ship be-fore God's throne. Here I stand, His child by His grace a - lone. The cross of Christ be - fore me as I praise His name on high. Here I stand on the Rock of Je - sus Christ. *Stanza:* The grace of God sur - rounds me, His good-ness and His love. Through faith a - lone in Je - sus, I'll live with Him a - bove. God's

# 5. Here I Stand—continued

Word is pure    and    ho - ly.    His    truth has made    me    free.    Here I

stand    in new life He's giv-en    me.                    Christ.

---

*For it is by grace you have been saved, through faith—and this not from yourselves, it is the gift of God—not by works, so that no one can boast. For we are God's workmanship, created in Christ Jesus to do good works, which God prepared in advance for us to do. Ephesians 2:8–10*

# 6. Who Was the Man

Katherine K. Davis

*"Come, follow Me," Jesus said, "and I will make you fishers of men."*
Matthew 4:19

# Who Was the Man

## Activities for Involving Children

("Who Was the Man" is found on page 20.)

The stanzas of this song contain a simple outline of Jesus' life as it is taught in the first three Gospels. Expand on this outline in these ways:

1. Have the students devise simple dramas, with or without costumes, to act out each stanza. Freeze the skits at their climax and interview each actor to find out what he or she knows about, sees, or feels about what is happening.

2. Provide art supplies and challenge the students to illustrate one of the stanzas, including more details than are in the song lyrics. Let each student show and describe his or her picture.

3. Use Bible reference books—concordances, dictionaries, and the like—to locate Bible passages that provide details for each stanza.

Provide a robe and sash for one singer who will sing Jesus' words in the last lines of each stanza as a solo. Let the singer lead the children around the room or building while singing the song, perhaps adding other children to the "parade" as the invitation to follow is extended at the end of each stanza.

Sing the final stanza. Invite the children to consider areas of their lives where Jesus could be calling them to follow Him. Have them write short prayers asking His help as they respond to His call.

# 7. Jesus Lights the Way

J. R.

John Roth

1. Je - sus lights the way, chas - ing dark - ness and gloom a - way.
2. Waves may roll and crash, thun - der rum - bles, and light - nings flash;
3. Come and join the song, praise the Sav - ior, whose light is strong.

Shin - ing like the sun, with love e - ter - nal for ev - 'ry - one. I'm
Seas may rage and storm, but in the har - bor I'm safe from harm; Re -
He will show the way, and bring you back when you go a - stray. Come

hap - py ev - 'ry day, with Je - sus light - ing the way.
joic - ing ev - 'ry day, with Je - sus light - ing the way.
join us as we pray, with Je - sus light - ing the way.

*Coda*

*When Jesus spoke again to the people, He said, "I am the light of the world. Whoever follows Me will never walk in darkness, but will have the light of life." John 8:12*

# Jesus Lights the Way

## Activities for Involving Children

("Jesus Lights the Way" is found on page 22.)

 This a great song for rhythm instruments. Distribute maracas, clappers, sandpaper blocks, rhythm sticks, and similar instruments and assign different rhythms to each instrument. (For example, rhythm sticks could tap on beat 1 of each measure, maracas could shake on beats 2 and 4, and sandpaper blocks could "swish" in the rhythm of the first measure of the bass line.)

 Have the children bring flashlights. Or distribute mini-flashlights, such as are found on key chains. Have the students turn on and wave the lights whenever they sing "Jesus lights the way" or "… with Jesus lighting the way."

Teach theses motions to accompany the lyrics as the children sing:

1. Jesus lights the way, *(Both hands overhead, slowly lower to sides in an arc.)*
    chasing darkness and gloom away; *(Right hand, then left hand behind back.)*
   Shining like the sun, *(Hands overhead, fingers spread.)*
    with love eternal for ev'ry one. *(Hands to opposite shoulders, then hands out, palms forward.)*
   I'm happy ev'ry day, *(Point to self with thumbs.)*
    with Jesus lighting the way. *(Both hands overhead, slowly lower to sides in an arc.)*

2. Waves may roll and crash, *(Make waves with arms.)*
    thunder rumbles, and lightnings flash; *(Simulate lightning bolts with hands.)*
   Seas may rage and storm, *(Shake fists.)*
    but in the harbor I'm safe from harm; *(Clasp hands.)*
   Rejoicing ev'ry day, *(Point to self with thumbs.)*
    with Jesus lighting the way. *(Both hands overhead, slowly lower to sides in an arc.)*

3. Come and join the song, *("Come here" gesture.)*
    praise the Savior, whose light is strong. *(Hands out, palms up; flex muscles.)*
   He will show the way, *(Arms extended.)*
    and bring you back when you go astray. *(Hands to opposite shoulders.)*
   Come join us as we pray, *(Hands folded.)*
    with Jesus lighting the way. *(Both hands overhead, slowly lower to sides in an arc.)*

# 8. Oh, Sing to the Lord

*(Cantad al Señor)*

Gerhard Cartford, tr.

Brazilian folk song

*Introduction*

1. Oh, sing to the Lord, Oh, sing God a new song.
*1. Can - tad al Se - ñor un cán - ti - co nue - vo,*
2. For God is the Lord, And God has done won - ders.
*2. Pues nues - tro Se - ñor ha he - cho pro - di - gios,*

Oh, sing to the Lord, Oh, sing God a new song.
*Can - tad al Se - ñor un cán - ti - co nue - vo,*
For God is the Lord, And God has done won - ders.
*Pues nues - tro Se - ñor ha he - cho pro - di - gios,*

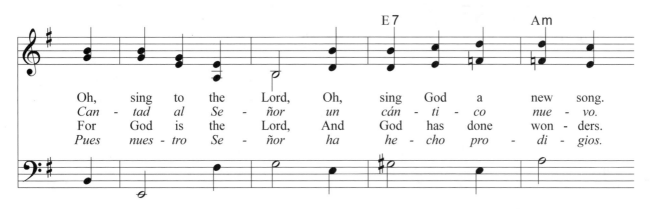

Oh, sing to the Lord, Oh, sing God a new song.
*Can - tad al Se - ñor un cán - ti - co nue - vo.*
For God is the Lord, And God has done won - ders.
*Pues nues - tro Se - ñor ha he - cho pro - di - gios.*

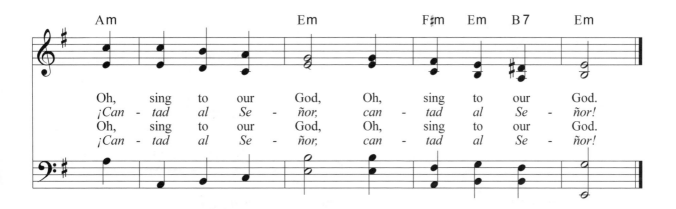

Oh, sing to our God, Oh, sing to our God.
*¡Can - tad al Se - ñor, can - tad al Se - ñor!*
Oh, sing to our God, Oh, sing to our God.
*¡Can - tad al Se - ñor, can - tad al Se - ñor!*

*Sing to the LORD a new song,*
*for He has done marvelous things.*
Psalm 98:1

# Oh, Sing to the Lord

## Activities for Involving Children
("Oh, Sing to the Lord" is found beginning on page 24.)

♪ Teach the children the Spanish words right along with the English ones. Both are translations from Portuguese, the predominant language in Brazil, where the song originated.

♪ Have the students find Psalm 98 in their Bibles. Invite the students to match the stanzas of the song with the psalm verses from which they are adapted. Ask the students to consider what circumstances in the lives of God's people might have inspired the psalm to be written. What circumstances might cause us to sing this song today?

♪ Compare the images of this song with those found in another familiar paraphrase of Psalm 98—"Joy to the World, the Lord Is Come," the popular Christmas hymn.

♪ Use drums in a light, driving rhythm ( ) as a background for singing. Provide the drummer(s) with a costume of sombrero and bandanna for greater effect.

# Awesome God

## Activities for Involving Children
("Awesome God" is found beginning on page 28.)

🌐 Discuss the messages communicated by the powerful images in the stanzas of this song:

**Stanza 1**—This stanza deals with the essence of Genesis 3. "Putting on the ritz" means being snobbish. When Adam and Eve sinned in the garden of Eden, God—in great love for His people—rescued them from living eternally with the consequences of their sin (see Genesis 3:22). He would provide His own Son as payment for sin. When Christ returns, all who by the Spirit's power have faith in Him will dwell with God eternally in heaven (John 3:16).

**Stanza 2**—This stanza goes back to Genesis 1 and 2, showing our God to be an all-powerful Creator, bringing all things to be out of nothing through His Word: "God said … and there was …" His is the power to judge and punish those who forget Him (Genesis 19; Isaiah 17:10–11), and His is the power to have mercy on those who turn to Him (Isaiah 45:22).

🌐 Study carefully one of the many psalms that describe God's reign (such as Psalm 9, 93, 97, or 99). Invite the children to find evidence of God's power—both in the psalm and in their world—and evidence of God's love for His people—again, both in the psalm and in their lives.

🌐 After the children have learned the song, select individuals or small groups to sing most of each stanza while the entire group joins in on the repeated phrase, "Our God is an awesome God," and on the refrain.

🌐 Challenge the group to invent actions to go with the lyrics.

# 9. Awesome God

R. M.

Rich Mullins

The LORD reigns,
    let the nations tremble
He sits enthroned between the cherubim,
    let the earth shake.

Great is the LORD in Zion;
    He is exalted over all the nations.
Let them praise Your great and awesome name—
    He is holy.
          Psalm 99:1–3

# 10. Greet the Rising Sun

Stephen P. Starke

*Le Ping*, Chinese folk tune
arranged by John Eggert

1. Greet the ris - ing sun, Shin - ing with bright force,
2. Fa - ther, hear my prayer, Keep me safe to - day;
3. Lord, I will to - day On Your love re - ly;

Like an ath - lete strong, Set to run the course.
Sanc - ti - fy my thoughts, All I do and say:
Let no e - vil thought Cloud the clear blue sky.

Birds soar high a - bove, Wild - flow'rs bloom be - low;
As I teach the young And es - teem the old,
Joy - ful and con - tent With life's sim - pler things,

With the day's new light, Glad to work I go.
May Your bount - eous grace By my life be told.
Know - ing all I need From Your kind - ness springs.

*And whatever you do, whether in word or deed, do it all in the name of the Lord Jesus, giving thanks to God the Father through Him.*
Colossians 3:17

# Greet the Rising Sun

## Activities for Involving Children

("Greet the Rising Sun" is found on page 30.)

Involve the students in a variety of instruments that will highlight this original oriental melody—flute or recorder (wooden flute); finger cymbals and chimes; xylophones, glockenspiels, and other instruments played with mallets. On the first, second, and fourth lines, various ostinato parts (repeated note patterns) can be devised using notes in the pentatonic scale (F, G, A, C, and D) repeated in one-, two-, or four-measure patterns. (The pentatonic scale can also be played by simply using the black keys on the piano.) For an ethereal sound, provide several students with small metal wind chimes; have them shake the chimes during the last measure of each line.

*Especially for boys:* Choreograph strong, flowing movements in the style of some forms of oriental martial arts. Avoid abrupt or violent movements that would be contrary to the peaceful nature of the song.

Take time to discuss the text and how it can apply to children the age of your students. "Glad to work I go" (at the end of stanza 1): Ask, "What is the 'work' of children?" (Chores, school and homework, living as good citizens, living as Christians; all of life can be seen as our work.) "As I teach the young and esteem the old" (stanza 2): Remind them that there are younger children who look up to them and learn from their example. They may also be mentors and teachers of younger siblings and other young children.

*Especially for girls:* Locate oriental fans—the larger, the better—and choreograph the song with slow, flowing movements.

# 11. Rise Up

J. F.

John Folkening

Rise up, rise up and fol-low Je-sus, your lead-er. Rise up, rise up and leave your old life be-hind. Rise up, rise up and start a won-der-ful jour-ney. 'Cause on-ly Je-sus knows what you'll

find.                Rise up,    rise up and trust in    Je - sus, your    lead - er.

Rise up,    rise up, He'll give you    faith to be - gin.        Rise up,    rise up, He'll give new

strength to your    bod - y.    But    best of    all, He'll free you from    sin.

Rise up, rise up and count on Je-sus, your lead-er. Rise up, rise up, and let Him han-dle each care. Rise up, rise up, the time has come to get start-ed. The truth is, it's a jun-gle out there. Rise up! Rise up! Rise up!

*Praise the LORD, O my soul,*
  *and forget not all His benefits—*
*who forgives all your sins*
  *and heals all your diseases,*

*who redeems your life from the pit*
  *and crowns you with love and compassion,*
*who satisfies your desires with good things*
  *so that your youth is renewed like the eagle's.*
    Psalm 103:2–5

# Rise Up

## Activities for Involving Children
("Rise Up" is found beginning on page 32.)

In a large group, create six smaller groups of singers. Assign two groups to each for the first three lines of each stanza. One group sings the first "Rise up," the second group sings the second "Rise up," and both groups sing the remainder of the line. (With fewer singers, create just two groups and let them sing all three lines in the manner described above.) Everyone sings the final line of each stanza. If you wish, have the students stand when they sing "Rise up," sit for the rest of each line, and stand on the last line of the stanza.

Teach these motions to accompany the singing.

Rise up, rise up and follow Jesus, your leader.
  *(March in place, slowly raise arms overhead.)*
Rise up, rise up and leave your old life behind.
  *(Slowly raise arms overhead; point with thumb behind you.)*
Rise up, rise up and start a wonderful journey.
  *(Slowly raise arms overhead.)*
'Cause only Jesus knows what you'll find.
  *(Stop all movement and sing.)*
Rise up, rise up and trust in Jesus, your leader.
  *(March in place, slowly raise arms overhead.)*
Rise up, rise up, He'll give you faith to begin.
  *(Slowly raise arms overhead; point up.)*
Rise up, rise up, He'll give new strength to your body.
  *(Slowly raise arms overhead.)*
But best of all, He'll free you from sin.
  *(Stop all movement and sing.)*
Rise up, rise up and count on Jesus, your leader.
  *(March in place, slowly raise arms overhead.)*
Rise up, rise up, and let Him handle each care.
  *(Slowly raise arms overhead.)*
Rise up, rise up, the time has come to get started.
  *(Slowly raise arms overhead.)*
The truth is, it's a jungle out there.
  *(Stop all movement and sing.)*
Rise up! Rise up! Rise up!
  *(Raise arms overhead three times)*

When singing this song for the congregation or an audience, create a visual impression of rising to a higher level with each stanza. For example, sit on the first stanza, kneel on the second, and stand on the third. On risers or steps, start with all the children on the floor in rows; with each stanza, or with each "Rise up ..." line, have the children step carefully back (and for some, up) a step.

# 12. We Are Marching in the Light of God

South African

*(Siyahamba)*

South African

God is light; in Him there is no darkness at all. … If we walk in the light, as He is in the light, we have fellowship with one another, and the blood of Jesus, His Son, purifies us from all sin. 1 John 1:5b, 7

But you are a chosen people, a royal priesthood, a holy nation, a people belonging to God, that you may declare the praises of Him who called you out of darkness into His wonderful light. 1 Peter 2:9

# We Are Marching in the Light of God

## Activities for Involving Children

("We Are Marching in the Light of God" is found beginning on page 36.)

To teach a simple version of this song, point out the A-A-B-B structure. (The first melody, A, is sung to the words "We are marching in the light of God, we are marching in the light of God." That line is then repeated. Then a new melody is introduced and repeated.) Teach everyone the melody (the top line), using the rhythm of the accompaniment on the B section and ignoring the "oo" part for now. *To add interest,* teach half of the singers (perhaps the girls) the sustained note and "oo" that begin the B section. *For advanced singers,* teach all four parts.

For additional stanzas, replace the word *marching* with other appropriate verbs, such as *singing, praying, living,* or *praying.*

Teach the students the African lyrics. (They are essentially phonetic.) First practice speaking the African text. Then chant that text in the rhythm of the song. Finally, sing it with the melody or in parts. Perhaps people you know can teach the children to sing this simple phrase—"We are marching in the light of God"—in other languages for an even broader cultural experience.

Add clapping, drums (especially conga drums), and other rhythm instruments.

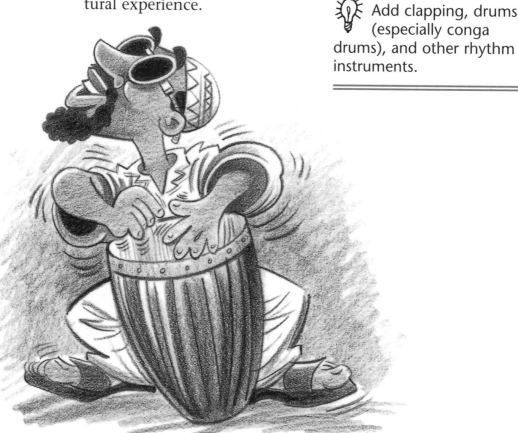

# I'm in the Same Boat with Jesus

## Activities for Involving Children

("I'm in the Same Boat with Jesus" is found beginning on page 40.)

Round up a pair of cool sunglasses for each child (or have the students bring their own) and encourage finger snapping to capture the blues feel of the song. Experiment with appropriate vocal styles.

Adapt appropriate dance steps into a line dance that all the children can do.

One or more of your students may be able to create a "hand jive" routine that students can do in pairs.

Have a serious discussion about the things that frighten young people (and adults, for that matter)—storms, dark streets, ominous strangers, serious illness, death—and the assurance of Jesus' constant presence and protection. You might have each student choose one such danger and illustrate it on paper or write a prayer asking for God's protection.

Discuss Hebrews 4:14–16. Invite children to list ways Jesus is like us and not like us.

SNAP

# 13. I'm in the Same Boat with Jesus

J. F.

John Folkening

1. A   boat   ride   in   a   storm
   storms   we   face   in   life

ain't   no   walk   through   the   park.
can   be   scar - y   and   wild;

The
I

waves   get   might - y   high,   the   sky   turns   oh,   so   dark.
feel   I'm   all   a - lone,   for - get   that   I'm   God's   child.

I'm   real - ly   glad   that   Je - sus   is   in   the   same   boat   with   me.

*"And surely I am with you always, to the very end of the age."*
Matthew 28:20

# 14. Hope's Celebration

(God Is My Fortress)

T.K.D.

Terry K. Dittmer

**Refrain:** God is my for-tress; I shall not be shak-en. God is my rock; He's my
**2nd time:** Je-sus Je-sus

sure foun-da-tion. God is my re-fuge; He's my soul's sal-va-tion. Hope's ce-le-bra-tion!
Je-sus

**2. To stanzas** *(To Coda after last refrains)*

**Stanzas** 1. En-e-mies threat-en. But God will tend them.
2. We stand for-giv-en, turned now toward heav-en.
3. Fa-ther, Cre-a-tor, al-might-y mak-er;

God does not fail us though storms as-sail us. God's love en-folds us. His
In-stru-ments sound-ing, drums loud-ly pound-ing, Cho-rus-es sing-ing, new
Je-sus, our broth-er, friend like no oth-er; Spir-it in-spires, light-

*D.S. al Coda* Coda

mer-cy holds us. Praise to the great Trin-i-ty! Al-le-lu-ia!
songs are ring-ing Praise to the great Trin-i-ty! Al-le-lu-ia!
ing faith's fires. Praise to the great Trin-i-ty! Al-le-lu-ia!

*Find rest, O my soul, in God alone; my hope comes from Him.*
*He alone is my rock and my salvation; He is my fortress, I will not be shaken. Psalm 62:5–6*

# Hope's Celebration

## Activities for Involving Children

("Hope's Celebration" is found on page 42.)

This spirited song lends itself to all kinds of dancing and movement. Experiment with circle dances, hand motions, "shimmies," clapping, and other means of getting the children moving.

Guide the children in an exploration of Psalm 62, on which the song is based. Match the phrases in the song with specific psalm verses. Or study Psalm 46, another psalm with a powerful "fortress" image.

- - - - - - - - - - - - - - - - - - - - - - - - - -

This is another song with great potential for choreographed motions to accompany the lyrics. Create your own or try these:

On the refrain: Roll arms for two beats, point left; roll arms, point right. (Repeat two more times, once for each line.) On last line, roll arms for two beats, throw arms up overhead on "celebration."

On the stanzas: First line—push down low with hands toward ground on first measure, then place hands on knees for second measure. Second line—hands on hips for one measure, hands pushed out in front for the second measure. Third line—hands hugging self on first measure, hands out to side with palms up on second measure. Last line—hands overhead, clap after "Trinity" and throw a fist in the air on "Alleluia!"

- - - - - - - - - - - - - - - - - - - - - - - - - -

# 15. My Shepherd and Forever Friend

L. G.

Lana Gibbons

Je - sus, Sav - ior, Shep - herd, Lord for - ev - er.

You are there to lead and love me like no oth - er can.

Je - sus, Sav - ior, Shep - herd, Lord for - ev - er.

1. You feed me with words so true, teach - ing me to talk like You,
2. You are there right at my side. In Your love I will a - bide.
3. In my weak - ness You are strong. You make right from all my wrong.

Love and live the way You do, My Shep - herd and for - ev - er Friend.
You shall al - ways be my Guide, My Shep - herd and for - ev - er Friend.
Teach - ing me my whole life long, My Shep - herd and for - ev - er Friend.

*My command is this: Love each other as I have loved you. Greater love has no one than this, that He lay down His life for His friends.* John 15:12–13

# My Shepherd and Forever Friend

## Activities for Involving Children
("My Shepherd and Forever Friend" is found on page 44.)

 Teach the girls the melody. Teach the boys the melody for the last four lines (where the words are different each stanza). For the first section, teach the boys this simple bass part:

You are my friend. You are my friend. You are my friend. You feed me with . . .

 In the first section, and on the last few words, have the students do hand motions as they sing.

**Jesus,**
(use middle finger to touch both palms in turn)

**Savior,**

**Shepherd,**

**Lord forever,**

**You are there**

**to lead and love me**

**like no other can.**

(Repeat "Jesus, Savior, Shepherd, Lord forever." Then no signs until ...)

**... my Shepherd**

**and forever Friend.**

# 16. Right from the Start

T. & N. S. S.

Todd and Nancy S. Stallard

*Let the name of the LORD be praised,*
*both now and forevermore.*
*From the rising of the sun to the place where it sets,*
*the name of the LORD is to be praised.*
Psalm 113:2–3

# Right from the Start

## Activities for Involving Children
("Right from the Start" is found on page 46.)

⭐ Let the children suggest words to sing in place of "praise" to add other stanzas to the song (*love, serve, thank, pray to, worship, honor, obey, follow,* and many others).

⭐ Challenge the students to shout words of praise during the brief space after the word "praise" (or its replacement) in each line of the song. Start with a one-syllable word such as "yea." Then try two syllables—"hooray"; "rejoice"; "go, God"; or "praise God." For a real challenge, try "Hallelujah."

⭐ Discuss the implications of the Bible verses printed below the song—Psalm 113:2–3, "From the rising of the sun to the place where it sets, the name of the LORD is to be praised." What does it mean to praise God from the very start of the day to the very end? How can Christians do this? (One great way is with singing!)

# 17. Here We Are Now

T. K.D.

Terry K. Dittmer

1. Fa - ther, Fa - ther, awe-some cre - a - tor, Won-der-ful God, our
2. Je - sus, Je - sus, beau - ti - ful broth - er, Gen-tle and kind, a
3. Spir - it, Spir - it, great sanc - ti - fi - er, Give us Your pow - er,
4. By Word, by grace, by faith all a-lone— These are the means by which

mar - vel - ous mak - er Leads us, guides us, shows us His way,
friend like no oth - er. On a cross He suf - fered to save us
set us on fire. Claim us, name us, e - quip and in - spire;
our God is known. Our God, our help, to all gen - er - a - tions;

# 17. Here We Are Now—continued

*If you confess with your mouth, "Jesus is Lord," and believe in your heart that God raised Him from the dead, you will be saved.* Romans 10:9

# Here We Are Now

## Activities for Involving Children
("Here We Are Now" is found beginning on page 48.)

△ Point out the themes of the first three stanzas of the song—Father, Jesus, and Spirit. Provide craft materials (construction paper, marking pens, Styrofoam shapes, toothpicks, craft sticks, tape, glue). Invite the students to create symbols of the Trinity—images or constructions that represent the three persons of God. Or let the students form teams of three, each one creating a symbol for one person of the Trinity. Play the recording of the song as the students work to inspire their efforts and help them learn the song.

△ Produce a music video. Bring a video camera to class. Brainstorm people or activities that could be recorded to reflect the message of each stanza and the refrain of the song (remember that the refrain is sung four times; use four ideas or tape the same activity four times). You may wish to record your group singing the song with the motions suggested below. Keep it simple by choosing just one activity for each part of the song. Record about 20 seconds of tape for each stanza and 20 seconds for each refrain. It is important to record the sections of your video program in order, unless you have means to edit the final tape. Sing the song as your final "music video" is shown.

# Shine, Jesus, Shine

## Activities for Involving Children

("Shine, Jesus, Shine" is found beginning on page 52.)

Invite the students to suggest biblical sources for the three images employed in the refrain—Jesus shining with the Father's glory, the Holy Spirit's fire, and the flood of God's grace and mercy (possibilities include the Transfiguration, Pentecost, and Baptism).

Let the students create pom-poms by rolling 12-inch widths of Mylar (shiny plastic film) into 1-inch tubes, taping about 4 inches of the seam at one end, and cutting the other 8 inches of the tube into ⅜-inch strips. As they sing, let the children wave their pom-poms whenever the words of the song refer to light (words such as *shine, glory, blaze, fire, light,* or *brightness*).

Invite the students to reflect on the words of stanza 2. Share these words from 2 Corinthians 3:18: "And we, who with unveiled faces all reflect the Lord's glory, are being transformed into His likeness with ever-increasing glory, which comes from the Lord, who is the Spirit." Use a flashlight and mirrors to demonstrate how light can be reflected; a mirror has no light of its own, but it can be as bright as a flashlight. So it is with Christians—we shine God's glory and love to the people around us, not by our own light, but as reflections of God's light that shines in us. Let the students experiment, reflecting the flashlight's beam from mirror to mirror, around corners, through "tunnels," into dark corners. Encourage the students to be mirrors of Christ's light.

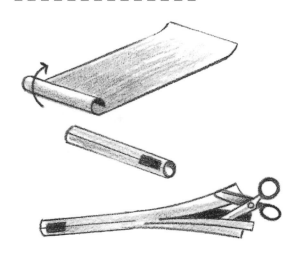

Provide each child with a flashlight (or have each child bring one). Use thin strips of dark tape (electrician's tape, duct tape, or masking tape) to create a cross in the middle of the clear lens of each flashlight or to block out all but a cross shape. Let the children "shine Jesus' cross" on the walls and ceilings of the darkened room as they sing or listen to the song.

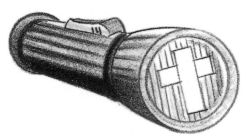

# 18. Shine, Jesus, Shine

Graham Kendrick                                                                 Graham Kendrick

# 18. Shine, Jesus, Shine—continued

in the midst of the dark - ness, shin - ing. Je - sus, light of the
so our fa - ces dis - play Your like - ness, Ev - er chang - ing from

world, shine up - on us, set us free by the truth You now bring us.
glo - ry to glo - ry, mir - rored here, may our lives tell Your sto - ry.

*To Refrain*

Shine on me, shine on me.
Shine on me, shine on me.

---

*For God, who said, "Let light shine out of darkness," made His light shine
in our hearts to give us the light of the knowledge of the glory of God in
the face of Christ. But we have this treasure in jars of clay to show that
this all-surpassing power is from God and not from us.*
2 Corinthians 4:6–7

# 19. Kids of the Kingdom

Ralph Torres

R. T.

1. Kids of the king - dom, that's what we are:
2. My name is_____; I love the Lord.
3. Kids of the king - dom, that's what we are:
4. Praise to the Fa - ther, praise to the Son,

kids of the king - dom, that's what we are.
My name is_____; I love the Lord.
kids of the king - dom, that's what we are.
praise to the Spir - it, the Three in One.

We love Je - sus; we love the Lord.
They love Je - sus; they love the Lord.
We love Je - sus; we love the Lord.
We love Je - sus; we love the Lord.

We love Je - sus; we love the Lord.
They love Je - sus; they love the Lord.
We love Je - sus; we love the Lord.
We love Je - sus; we love the Lord.

*How great is the love the Father has lavished on us, that we should be called children of God! And that is what we are!* 1 John 3:1

**54**

# Kids of the Kingdom

## Activities for Involving Children
("Kids of the Kingdom" is found on page 54.)

 Note that stanza 2 has a blank space in the first two lines where children can sing their names. In a small group, with someone playing the accompaniment, these two lines can simply be repeated until every child has had a turn singing one of the lines with his or her name. In a large group, or with the recorded accompaniment, have the children sing their names simultaneously (first name, then last name—or first name, then "Christian").

 The repeated lines that end each stanza are natural places for a crescendo, climaxing on the word "Je-SUS." Experiment with ways to dramatize these crescendos—moving arms from down at one's sides to overhead, moving from a kneeling position to a standing position, and the like.

 The song lends itself to antiphonal singing, one group singing the first and third lines of each stanza and one group singing the second and fourth. Work on memorizing this song for easy group singing.

# 20. Our Hero

J. B.

Joanne Burns

1. Je - sus is the one who saves us. Je - sus is our heal - er too.
2. In Christ's love we live for - ev - er. God's truth comes to set us free.

Je - sus is the one who res - cues; Gave His life for me and you.
Sin and death have been de - feat - ed. Je - sus is our vic - to - ry!

**Refrain**

He is our he - ro. Christ is our he - ro. Love is His pow - er. Love is His

might. He is our he - ro; Christ is our he - ro. He is the way, the truth, the life.

*Grace and peace to you from God our Father and the Lord Jesus Christ, who gave Himself for our sins to rescue us from the present evil age, according to the will of our God and Father, to whom be glory for ever and ever. Amen. Galatians 1:3–5*

# Our Hero

## Activities for Involving Children
("Our Hero" is found on page 56.)

✌ "Hero" may be a lost concept in today's society. Take time to discuss what a hero is and does. You might include fairy-tale heroes, knights in shining armor, war heroes, cartoon superheroes, and the like. Ask, "Who are the world's heroes today? Whom do people look up to or count on for help? What are the problems with the world's heroes?" (They either are not perfect and may fail us, or they are not real.) "In what way is Jesus greater than any of the heroes we have talked about?" (He is perfect and real; He rescues us for all eternity from physical and spiritual death.)

✌ Once the students have learned the song, use these techniques to further engage them: (1) sing the stanzas antiphonally, one half of the students singing the first and third lines and the other half singing the second and fourth lines, or use a soloist on lines one and three; (2) challenge the students to create additional verses, perhaps based on the hero discussion above ("Greater than a superhero, greater than the army's best …"); (3) divide the singers into two groups and sing the refrain in canon two beats apart (the second group sings "He …" just after the first group sings the first syllable of "… he-[ro] …").

✌ Teach these actions to accompany, and help students learn, the words:

1. Jesus is the one who saves us. *(Pretend to pull a rope.)*
Jesus is our healer too. *(Pretend to put on a bandage.)*
Jesus is the one who rescues; *(Make cross with fingers.)*
Gave His life for me and you. *(Point to self, others.)*

He is our hero. Christ is our hero. *(Sway with arms above head.)*
Love is His power. Love is His might. *(Flex right biceps; flex left biceps.)*
He is our hero; Christ is our hero. *(Sway with arms above head.)*
He is the way, the truth, the life. *(Point to heaven; touch lips with finger; make cross with fingers.)*

2. In Christ's love we live forever. *(Draw outline of heart with fingers.)*
God's truth comes to set us free. *(Pretend to break a chain from around neck.)*
Sin and death have been defeated. *(Flex muscles.)*
Jesus is our victory! *(Make V with fingers, point up.)*

# Lyrics

## 1. Celebrate Jesus!

### Lisa Hahn

*Refrain:* Let's celebrate (come on and celebrate),
Let's celebrate (sing to Jesus),
Let's celebrate (shout for joy and)—
Celebrate Jesus!

1. Sing to Him, you joyful ones;
Make music, play, and shout.
He's made you righteous in His sight,
So let your praise come out! *Refrain*

2. By His Word the earth was formed;
He made the sea and sky.
He sent His Son to pay for sin
So we can live on high. *Refrain*

3. His love for us doesn't end.
His words are right and true.
A love that will not fail or fade—
A love for me and you! *Refrain*

4. So we wait in hope for Him;
Our help and shield He'll be.
In Him our hearts rejoice and sing
'Cause Christ has set us free! *Refrain*

Copyright © 1999 Concordia Publishing House.

## 2. Don't Look Back

### Lana Gibbons

1. Don't look back; Keep pressin' on.
Don't look back; Keep pressin' on.
Don't look back; Keep pressin' on.
On Jesus Christ I fix my eyes.
I'm heaven bound to win my prize *(clap, clap)*.
Don't look back *(clap, clap)*; Keep pressin' on.

2. Come with me; Keep pressin' on.
Come with me; Keep pressin' on.
Come with me; Keep pressin' on.
On Jesus Christ I fix my eyes.
I'm heaven bound to win my prize *(clap, clap)*.
Come with me *(clap, clap)*; Keep pressin' on.

3. Heav'n is home; Keep pressin' on.
Heav'n is home; Keep pressin' on.
Heav'n is home; Keep pressin' on.
On Jesus Christ I fix my eyes.
I'm heaven bound to win my prize *(clap, clap)*.
Heav'n is home *(clap, clap)*; Keep pressin' on.

4. Don't look back; Keep pressin' on.
Don't look back; Keep pressin' on.
Don't look back; Keep pressin' on.
On Jesus Christ I fix my eyes.
I'm heaven bound to win my prize *(clap, clap)*.
Don't look back *(clap, clap)*; Keep pressin' on.

Copyright © 1990 Lana Gibbons. Used by permission.

## 3. Come and Glorify the Name

### Dana Mengel

Come and glorify the name of Jesus.
Come exalt His name on high.
Come and sing His glory in the morning light;
In the night, all His mighty pow'r proclaim.
Alleluia, alleluia!
Alleluia, we sing!
Alleluia, alleluia,
Alleluia, to the King!
(To the King!)

Copyright © 1999 Concordia Publishing House.

# 4. Make Me Like You

Lana Gibbons

1. Jesus, Jesus, make me like You.
Make me to walk and to talk like You do.
Make my ears listen and make my heart new.
Jesus, make me be more like You.

2. Jesus, Jesus, make me like You.
Make me to touch and to care like You do.
Make me reach out with Your arms that forgive.
Jesus, make me live like You live.

3. Jesus, Jesus, make me like You.
Make me to love and to help like You do.
Make my eyes open so others can see.
Jesus, make Your love seen through me.

4. Jesus, Jesus, make me like You.
Make me to think and to do what You do.
Make me to serve You, give thanks and obey.
Jesus, make me like You today.

Copyright © 1999 Lana Gibbons. Used by permission.

# 5. Here I Stand

Lana Gibbons

*Refrain:*  Here I stand in worship before God's
throne.
Here I stand, His child by His grace
alone.
The cross of Christ before me
as I praise His name on high.
Here I stand on the Rock of Jesus
Christ.

The grace of God surrounds me, His goodness
and His love.
Through faith alone in Jesus, I'll live
with Him above,
God's Word is pure and holy.
His truth has made me free.
Here I stand in new life He's given me. *Refrain*

Copyright © 1997 Lana Gibbons. Used by permission.

# 6. Who Was the Man

Katherine K. Davis

1. Oh, who was the man,
two thousand years ago,
Who walked in Galilee,
Who said to the fishermen mending their nets,
"Rise up and follow Me.
Oh, rise up and follow, rise up and follow,
Rise up and follow Me"?

2. They followed Him down through village
and town,
And wondered at the words He said
As He healed the lame and the sick
and the blind,
And even raised the dead.
"Oh, rise up and follow, rise up and follow,
Rise up and follow Me."

3. They followed Him into a garden at night,
Then up to a cross on the hill;
And when He was laid in a stony tomb,
They seemed to hear Him still.
"Oh, rise up and follow, rise up and follow,
Rise up and follow Me."

4. That man who arose from the stony tomb
Is here and alive today.
Like friends you could meet on a crowded street,
And still you hear Him say,
"Oh, rise up and follow, rise up and follow,
Rise up and follow Me."

Copyright © 1971 Choristers Guild. Used by permission.

# 7. Jesus Lights the Way

## John Roth

1. Jesus lights the way,
    chasing darkness and gloom away;
Shining like the sun,
    with love eternal for ev'ryone.
I'm happy ev'ry day, with Jesus lighting the way.

2. Waves may roll and crash,
    thunder rumbles, and lightnings flash;
Seas may rage and storm,
    but in the harbor I'm safe from harm;
Rejoicing ev'ry day, with Jesus lighting the way.

3. Come and join the song,
    praise the Savior, whose light is strong.
He will show the way,
    and bring you back when you go astray.
Come join us as we pray, with Jesus lighting
    the way.

Copyright © 1998 Concordia Publishing House.

# 8. Oh, Sing to the Lord
## (Cantad al Señor)

## Gerhard Cartford, tr.
### Brazilian folk song

1. Oh, sing to the Lord, Oh, sing God a new song.
Oh, sing to the Lord, Oh, sing God a new song.
Oh, sing to our God, Oh, sing to our God.

2. For God is the Lord, And God has done wonders.
For God is the Lord, And God has done wonders.
For God is the Lord, And God has done wonders.
Oh, sing to our God, Oh, sing to our God.

1. *Cantad al Señor un cántico nuevo.*
*Cantad al Señor un cántico nuevo.*
*Cantad al Señor un cántico nuevo.*
*¡Cantad al Señor, cantad al Señor!*

2. *Pues nuestro Señor ha hecho prodigios,*
*Pues nuestro Señor ha hecho prodigios,*
*Pues nuestro Señor ha hecho prodigios.*
*¡Cantad al Señor, cantad al Señor!*

Copyright © Gerhard Cartford. Used by permission.

# 9. Awesome God

## Rich Mullins

Lyrics for "Awesome God" may not be reproduced without specific permission from BMG Songs or under the provisions of a CCLI (Christian Copyright Licensing, Inc.) agreement.

Contact BMG Songs at
1400 18th Avenue South
Nashville, TN 37212
or call 1-615-858-1332

Contact CCLI at
17201 NE Sacramento Street
Portland, OR 97230

# 10. Greet the Rising Sun

## Stephen P. Starke

1. Greet the rising sun,
Shining with bright force,
Like an athlete strong,
Set to run the course.
Birds soar high above,
Wildflow'rs bloom below;
With the day's new light,
Glad to work I go.

2. Father, hear my prayer,
Keep me safe today;
Sanctify my thoughts,
All I do and say:
As I teach the young
And esteem the old,
May Your bounteous grace
By my life be told.

3. Lord, I will today
On Your love rely;
Let no evil thought
Cloud the clear blue sky.
Joyful and content
With life's simpler things,
Knowing all I need
From Your kindness springs.

# 11. Rise Up

## John Folkening

Rise up, rise up and follow Jesus, your leader.
Rise up, rise up and leave your old life behind.
Rise up, rise up and start a wonderful journey.
'Cause only Jesus knows what you'll find.
Rise up, rise up and trust in Jesus, your leader.
Rise up, rise up He'll give you faith to begin.
Rise up, rise up, He'll give new strength
     to your body.
But best of all, He'll free you from sin.
Rise up, rise up and count on Jesus, your leader.
Rise up, rise up and let Him handle each care.
Rise up, rise up, the time has come
     to get started.
The truth is, it's a jungle out there.
Rise up! Rise up! Rise up!

# 12. We Are Marching in the Light of God

*(Siyahamba)*

## South African

We are marching in the light of God,
    we are marching in the light of God.
We are marching in the light of God,
    we are marching in the light of God.
We are marching, marching,
    we are marching, marching, (oo)
    we are marching in the light of God.
We are marching, marching,
    we are marching, marching, (oo)
    we are marching in the light of God.

*Siyahamb' ekukhanyen' kwenkhos',*
    *siyahamb' ekukhanyen' kwenkhos'.*
*Siyahamb' ekukhanyen' kwenkhos',*
    *siyahamb' ekukhanyen' kwenkhos'.*
*Siyahamba, hamba,*
    *siyahamba, hamba, (oo)*
    *siyahamb' ekukhanyen' kwenkhos'.*
*Siyahamba, hamba,*
    *siyahamba, hamba, (oo)*
    *siyahamb' ekukhanyen' kwenkhos'.*

## 13. I'm in the Same Boat with Jesus

### John Folkening

1. A boat ride in a storm
     ain't no walk through the park.
The waves get mighty high,
     the sky turns oh, so dark.
I'm really glad that Jesus
     is in the same boat with me.
I'm in the same boat with Jesus,
     and that's where I want to be.
I'm in the same boat with Jesus,
     no matter how rough the sea.
'Cause Jesus won't let me sink,
     He proved it on Calvary.

2. The storms we face in life
     can be scary and wild;
I feel I'm all alone,
     forget that I'm God's child.
I'm really glad that Jesus
     is in the same boat with me.
I'm in the same boat with Jesus,
     and that's where I want to be.
I'm in the same boat with Jesus,
     no matter how rough the sea.
'Cause Jesus won't let me sink,
     He proved it on Calvary.

## 14. Hope's Celebration

(God Is My Fortress)
### Terry K. Dittmer

*Refrain:*  God (Jesus) is my fortress;
     I shall not be shaken.
     God (Jesus) is my rock;
     He's my sure foundation.
     God (Jesus) is my refuge;
     He's my soul's salvation.
     Hope's celebration!

1. Enemies threaten. But God will tend them.
God does not fail us though storms assail us.
God's love enfolds us. His mercy holds us.
Praise to the great Trinity! Alleluia! *Refrain*

2. We stand forgiven, turned now
     toward heaven.
Instruments sounding, drums loudly pounding,
Choruses singing, new songs are ringing.
Praise to the great Trinity! Alleluia! *Refrain*

3. Father, Creator, almighty maker;
Jesus, our brother, friend like no other;
Spirit inspires, lighting faith's fires.
Praise to the great Trinity! Alleluia! *Refrain*

## 15. My Shepherd and Forever Friend

**Lana Gibbons**

1. Jesus, Savior, Shepherd, Lord forever.
You are there to lead and love me
    like no other can.
Jesus, Savior, Shepherd, Lord forever.
You feed me with words so true,
Teaching me to talk like You.
Love and live the way You do,
My Shepherd and forever Friend.

2. Jesus, Savior, Shepherd, Lord forever.
You are there to lead and love me
    like no other can.
Jesus, Savior, Shepherd, Lord forever.
You are there right at my side.
In Your love I will abide.
You shall always be my Guide,
My Shepherd and forever Friend.

3. Jesus, Savior, Shepherd, Lord forever.
You are there to lead and love me
    like no other can.
Jesus, Savior, Shepherd, Lord forever.
In my weakness You are strong.
You make right from all my wrong.
Teaching me my whole life long,
My Shepherd and forever Friend.

4. Jesus, Savior, Shepherd, Lord forever.
You are there to lead and love me
    like no other can.
Jesus, Savior, Shepherd, Lord forever.
You were there right from my start,
Living in me, in my heart;
Holding me when I depart,
My Shepherd and forever Friend.

5. Jesus, Savior, Shepherd, Lord forever.
You are there to lead and love me
    like no other can.
Jesus, Savior, Shepherd, Lord forever.
In my place it's You that died—
Love outpoured, so deep, so wide.
So in heav'n I'll live beside
My Shepherd and forever Friend.

## 16. Right from the Start

**Todd and Nancy S. Stallard**

I will praise the Lord all day long.
I will praise the Lord with my song.
I will praise the Lord with all my heart.
I will praise the Lord right from the start.

## 17. Here We Are Now

**Terry K. Dittmer**

1. Father, Father, awesome creator,
Wonderful God, our marvelous maker
Leads us, guides us, shows us His way,
Lovingly blesses each one of our days.

*Refrain:*  Here we are now!
    Our faith we're confessing.
    Here we are now!
    Our love we're expressing.
    Here we are now, sent forth
      by God's blessing.
    Thankfully our praises we bring
      unto God, our heavenly King!

2. Jesus, Jesus, beautiful brother,
Gentle and kind, a friend like no other,
On a cross He suffered to save us
And upon Easter, new life He gave us. *Refrain*

3. Spirit, Spirit, great sanctifier,
Give us Your power, set us on fire.
Claim us, name us, equip and inspire;
Show us our place in the heavenly choir. *Refrain*

4. By Word, by grace, by faith all alone—
These are the means by which our God is known.
Our God, our help, to all generations;
God is the reason for celebration! *Refrain*

# 18. Shine, Jesus, Shine

**Graham Kendrick**

*Refrain:* Shine, Jesus, shine,
          fill this land with the Father's glory;
Blaze, Spirit, blaze,
          set our hearts on fire.
Flow, river, flow,
          flood the nations with love and mercy;
Send forth Your Word, Lord,
          and let there be light!

1. Lord, the light of Your love is shining;
       in the midst of the darkness, shining.
Jesus, light of the world, shine upon us,
       set us free by the truth You now bring us.
Shine on me, shine on me. *Refrain*

2. As we gaze on Your kingly brightness,
       so our faces display Your likeness,
Ever changing from glory to glory,
       mirrored here, may our lives tell Your story.
Shine on me, shine on me. *Refrain*

# 19. Kids of the Kingdom

**Ralph Torres**

# 20. Our Hero

**Joanne Burns**

1. Jesus is the one who saves us.
Jesus is our healer too.
Jesus is the one who rescues;
Gave His life for me and you.

*Refrain:* He is our hero. Christ is our hero.
          Love is His power. Love is His might.
          He is our hero; Christ is our hero.
          He is the way, the truth, the life.

2. In Christ's love we live forever.
God's truth comes to set us free.
Sin and death have been defeated.
Jesus is our victory! *Refrain*